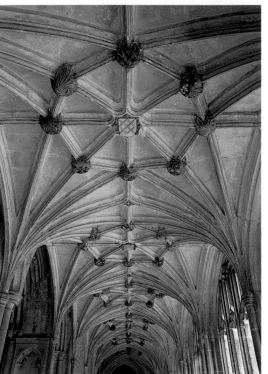

Lacock Abbey

Wiltshire

THE NATIONAL TRUST

Images of past and present

At Lacock, you get a keen sense of the continuity and connectedness of English life. It is a place where the past and present meet, where all the elements – house, grounds, church, village and people – fit together.

Today, Lacock may seem like a picturesque backwater, isolated from the modern world, but at many periods in its history its owners have been in the forefront of both art and science.

Still at the core of Lacock Abbey is the cloister of the Augustinian nunnery founded in 1232 by *Ela, Countess of Salisbury*. Ela also helped to found Salisbury Cathedral, whose 123-metre-high spire is one of the engineering wonders of the Middle Ages. In 1215 her husband, William Longespée, had witnessed the signing of the Magna Carta, which for the first time limited royal power by written decree.

From 1540 *William Sharington* transformed Lacock into a country house. He retained much of the medieval building, but added an octagonal tower in the new Renaissance style, which has survived remarkably untouched, both inside and out.

In the 1750s, *John Ivory Talbot* was inspired by Lacock's medieval origins to rebuild the Hall in the Gothick style – a forerunner of the Gothic Revival that was to sweep over Britain in the 19th century.

William Henry Fox Talbot was one of the greatest of all the great Victorians. At Lacock in the 1830s, he pioneered photography as art, science and commercial technology. This guide, and every other book and magazine illustrated with photographs, would be impossible without the discoveries made by Fox Talbot at Lacock. Fox Talbot

William Sharington   *John Ivory Talbot*   *William Henry Fox Talbot*   *Matilda Talbot*

took thousands of photographs, which provide a fascinating and beautiful record of Lacock in his time. Lacock today is more photographed than ever as an appropriate setting for numerous historical dramas on film and television.

Matilda Talbot, the last private owner of Lacock, sold paintings from the house, but preserved its rich archive, and generously gave the abbey, the village and the rest of the estate to the National Trust in 1944 so that they might all remain intact and together. Her family still live in the house, keeping the place alive. As the direct descendants of the Sharingtons, they also maintain that link between past and present which is the special appeal of Lacock.

*Lacock Abbey about 1844;
a calotype by Fox Talbot*

The clock-tower in the Tudor Stable Court is framed in the Gothick arch commissioned by John Ivory Talbot

Tour of the Abbey

The Hall

This entrance hall was created in 1754–5 for John Ivory Talbot by his architect, Sanderson Miller. It is an early, and little altered, example of the Gothick style, the first phase of the Gothic Revival.

Ivory Talbot demolished the Tudor hall previously on this site, which he dismissed as 'Horrid!' All that he preserved from the old hall was the *medieval stained glass*, which he placed in a new rose window over the entrance door and in the large Gothic windows flanking it. Ivory Talbot specified that the doorcases, windows and chimneypiece in his new hall should be 'in the Gothic Taste'. Miller supplied all these, together with a Gothick cornice and canopied wall niches.

The chimneypiece is carved from Painswick limestone with an abbess's mitre and veiled crosiers in memory of the founder and first abbess of Lacock, Ela, Countess of Salisbury, whose figure appears immediately above. It also incorporates 17th-century work in the side panels.

The brass firedogs, *c.*1680, were a present to Ivory Talbot from Lady Dacre, given in 1757 at Miller's suggestion.

'Notwithstanding its size, 50 feet long by 30 feet broad by 36 feet high, it is a friendly room and is moreover wonderfully adaptable. It will accommodate 250 guests, and we have more than once had that number at family weddings; yet if only two or three of us are sitting there by the great fireplace, we feel quite cosy and intimate, with no sense of having been left in the town hall.'

Matilda Talbot

In 1756 *the barrel ceiling* was painted with the coats of arms of Ivory Talbot's friends and relations, perhaps inspired by the medieval armorial decoration in the cloister vaulting. He called the result 'the delight of all eyes', and was keen to baptise his new hall with a party, 'when all my friends who are in the country and whose arms are emblazoned on the ceiling will do me the honour of their company and a grand sacrifice to Bacchus will be the consequence.'

The rose window over the entrance door contains fragments of reused medieval stained glass

Sculpture

The terracotta figures in the wall niches are the
most unusual feature of the room. They are
the work of Victor Alexander Sederbach, an
Austrian or south German modeller or stove-
maker, who produced them at Lacock between
May 1755 and January 1756. The exact
programme is still unclear, but the figures
certainly include Ela, Countess of Salisbury
(over the fireplace), and probably her husband,
William Longespée, Earl of Salisbury (wearing
an earl's coronet and holding the plan of a
church: he founded Salisbury Cathedral); their
sons, William (in armour: he died on the
Crusades) and Nicholas (in mitre: he was a
bishop); and two of their granddaughters, who
were nuns at Lacock. There are also symbolic
representations of death (a skeleton) and
perhaps the seasons. The flamboyantly
Baroque style of the figures is a little incon-
gruous in a Gothick room, but evidently
pleased Ivory Talbot. He recommended
Sederbach to friends, but nothing else by this
mysterious sculptor is known.

Furniture

The four mid-18th-century yew-wood tables
were probably ordered by Ivory Talbot
specially for this room, as they are in a
matching Gothick style. *The hall-chairs* are
of the same date. This kind of chair was
deliberately not upholstered, to make it more
hard-wearing and to discourage casual visitors
from lingering.

The smaller organ is typical of English
chamber organs of *c.*1800. *The larger organ,*
*c.*1820, was bought from the eminent
organist, the late Lady Jeans. There is a long
tradition of music-making at Lacock.

Take the door in the right-hand wall to reach the
Dining Room.

(Left) Victor Alexander Sederbach's terracotta sculpture
of a winged and crowned skeleton probably symbolises
death. Its exact meaning remains a mystery

(Right) The terracotta sculpture of the scapegoat was
modelled by Sederbach. The sugar lump was first placed
on the goat's nose by a student in 1919

The Dining Room

The classical style of this room is in marked contrast to the Gothick Hall. It began life as part of the abbess's private quarters, and took its present form in the early 18th century, slightly before the Hall was created. Although it is a long way from the kitchen, the family continued to eat here every day until 1916, as they still do on special occasions.

On 11 October 1729 a grand dinner was held to celebrate the coming-of-age of Ivory Talbot's niece, Mary Elizabeth Davenport. There were three courses, the first comprising no fewer than eight separate dishes, which were all placed on the table at the same time, like a Chinese meal. These included boiled goose with celery sauce, fricassee of rabbit and veal ragout. The second course included partridge, duck and carp with kidney beans and almond cheesecake. For the dessert course, a central pyramid of wet and dry sweetmeats was surrounded by fruit, jellies, syllabubs and creams.

William Henry Fox Talbot generally diluted his after-dinner port with water. Puzzled that on one occasion his drink seemed to be getting stronger rather than weaker, he discovered that he had absentmindedly been adding gin rather than water. According to Matilda Talbot, meals were 'rather solemn' in the 1870s, at the end of

The Arts, after Cornelis van Haarlem, 1605

Over the fireplace is an allegorical portrait of the Dutch shell collector Jan Govertsz. van der Aar (1544/5–1612). He is shown seated, holding one of his shells. The other figures represent his artistic interests: music, painting and sculpture. Presiding over the company on the left is the naked figure of Peace (the olive branch) and Plenty (cornucopia). The destructive weapons of war (at the bottom left) have been laid aside. The picture has suffered in the distant past from aggressive cleaning.

Fox Talbot's life: 'There was a butler and a footman handing round dishes and nobody spoke much. Some dish was handed to me once that I didn't like, so I said, "No thank you, I hate that." My grandmother frowned, and said, "You should not speak like that; if you don't want a thing you must say 'I dislike it', not 'I hate it'."'

Fox Talbot's son, Charles, a fragile scholar, 'always had rather light food for lunch, minced veal or fish or something of that kind, especially made for him, but Aunt Rosamond and I usually had something else, for there were quite a number of ordinary dishes which he was afraid to eat in case they disagreed with him.'

Unusually among country-house owners, Matilda Talbot had trained as a professional cook. She always enjoyed cooking, but disliked the fancier recipes she was taught: 'It was very wearisome to bone larks with a small penknife, and anyhow it seemed a bad idea to eat larks instead of keeping them for their song.'

The room still has its original oak floor,

which encouraged Matilda Talbot to begin using this as a ballroom in 1916. She was always a welcoming host, although her parties were 'lamentably teetotal', according to one guest.

Pictures

Over the entrance door is an octagonal copy of Michael Dahl's portrait of *John Ivory Talbot*, the creator of this room and the Hall. The frame was originally made for a Holbein portrait of Henry VIII, now sold. The other paintings are mainly copies of mythological subjects by Rubens and portraits by his greatest pupil, Van Dyck, including (flanking entrance door) *Charles I out hunting* and *The Duchess of Richmond as St Agnes*.

Furniture

The fine Rococo pier-table and mirror between the windows on the wall facing the fireplace were supplied in 1750 by the Marlborough cabinet-maker Henry Hill, who also carved the fireplace and the frieze. *The white ceramic greyhounds* flanking the fireplace are Italian.

The South Gallery

This long room lies over the south side of the abbey cloister, originally connecting the abbess's private quarters and her chapel (at the west end), and running alongside the nave of the abbey church (now gone). Sharington converted it into a narrow two-room gallery with three windows on either side. The floor was covered with tiles bearing the Sharington cipher (examples on display in the Short Lobby).

In 1828–30 Fox Talbot created the present room by removing an 18th-century fireplace, adding the bay at the far end and raising the height of the ceiling. He also replaced the earlier windows with deep bay windows (oriels). The Wilton carpet is a 1968 copy of the Brussels carpet laid here in 1850 for the wedding of Fox Talbot's half-sister, Horatia.

According to Matilda Talbot, in the late 19th century 'my grandmother used this as her drawing-room, and here my great-aunts [Horatia and Caroline], who were both very musical, used to play harp and piano duets, and to sing.'

'One of these bay windows is so large that it makes a kind of drawing room where there are tables, sofas etc etc. The two others are much smaller; however they form recesses, and in each is a writing table where one can sit very comfortably without being seen by anyone in the Gallery. In fact it makes a very large, comfortable and artistic room.'

Amélina Petit de Billier,
11 September 1831

Pictures

Between the oriel windows on the right are portraits of Sir John Talbot (1630–1714) and his second wife, Barbara Slingsby. In 1668 Talbot fought in the most notorious duel of the 17th century, as second to the Earl of Shrewsbury, who was murdered in the skirmish by the 2nd Duke of Buckingham. Talbot himself was badly wounded.

The South Gallery

On the opposite wall is John Ivory Talbot's brother-in-law, Henry Davenport (1677–1731) as a young man. To the left is his son, Sharington Davenport, with his wife, Gratiana Rodd. The large conversation pieces further down the left wall depict seven of Sharington Davenport's children (No. 102) and him with his shooting companions (No. 101). They are on loan from a descendant.

Also on the left wall is Sir William Sharington (c.1495–1553; No. 19), who acquired Lacock Abbey in 1540 and converted it into a fashionable country house, building the octagonal tower. In the bay window opposite is displayed

The 19th-century Venetian glass chandelier

The birthplace of modern photography

The central bay window appears in one of the most famous images in the history of photography. In 1835 Fox Talbot managed to capture this view on a postage-stamp-sized negative, which is now recognised as the oldest in existence. This print was taken from it and hangs to the right of the window.

the pardon he received in 1549 after the fall of the Seymours (see p. 38). Over the fireplace is a copy of Van Dyck's famous portrait of the children of Charles I (No. 25). Hanging on the far left wall is Sir Gilbert Talbot (c.1606–95; No. 20), the younger brother of Sharington Talbot. From 1634 to 1645 he served with the English legation in Venice, running up debts of £13,000. A contemporary called him 'a great cheat at bowls and cards, not born to a farthing'. Despite this, he was elected a founder member of the Royal Society in 1663.

The *View of Lacock Abbey* on the easel was painted in March 1942 by John Piper, who paid a visit while he was recording the bomb damage in nearby Bath. He noted in his diary: 'LCC School in residence, and some paying guests. Miss Talbot efficient, with an office…. Peeling yellow plaster, dampening stonework, trestle tables sagging under dusty fragments.'

Ceramics

Some of the Meissen porcelain in the glass-fronted cabinet is recorded in an early photograph by Fox Talbot, a copy of which hangs nearby.

Glass

The chandelier is 19th-century Venetian coloured glass.

The Blue Parlour

The room was remodelled in the early 18th century by Sir John Talbot's second wife, Barbara; her portrait can be seen in the South Gallery. She installed the panelling, the chimneypiece and the sash-windows, which are set in stone mullions first inserted by Sir William Sharington. The room was later converted into a library.

After 1916 the bookcases were removed to reveal the panelling, which was repainted blue – the shade mixed by the village house painter. The colour was later found to resemble the original, as recorded in an 1829 watercolour. 'This was very satisfactory', Matilda Talbot agreed.

Pictures

The portraits include, left of the fireplace, (No. 33) John Talbot, the son of John Ivory Talbot. It was painted in Bath in the 1760s by

'I played the harp, the duet from the *Barber of Seville*; that from *la Donna del Lago*, with Horatia, and sang with the poet [the Irish writer Thomas Moore] Mozart's *Deli prendi un dolce amplesso*, from *la Clemenza di Tito*. We tried next some fragments of that admirable! three times admirable!!! *Requiem* of Mozart. He sang a melody *The Evening Song*, full of poetry and sentiment. He was always pleasant.'

Amélina Petit de Billier,
10 December 1827

the city's most fashionable artist, Thomas Gainsborough. The man in the blue coat (No. 43), right of the door in the far wall, is the gentleman-architect Sanderson Miller, who designed the Gothick Hall for Ivory Talbot.

Furniture

The 'Angel' harp was made in 1815 by Sébastien Erard and bought for Lacock in 1827. It was played most frequently by Mlle Amélina Petit de Billier, who lived at Lacock for many years as governess and companion, first to Fox Talbot's two half-sisters, and then to his three daughters.

The other furniture is mainly 18th-century English and oriental lacquer. *The cabinet on an ornate Charles II period stand* is probably Italian. *The Carlton House desk* was given by Queen Victoria to William Davenport Talbot to pay a debt incurred by her father, the Duke of Kent. This type of writing-desk is named after the London house occupied by the Prince Regent before he became king. *The small ebony- and rosewood-veneered cabinet* by the door to the Painting Room once belonged to the Pre-Raphaelite painter Dante Gabriel Rossetti.

Sculpture

On the Carlton House desk is *a bronze bust of Amy Burnett-Brown*, the grandmother of the late Anthony Burnett-Brown, Matilda Talbot's great-nephew, who lived at Lacock until his death in 2002.

Fox Talbot's half-sister Horatia playing the Erard harp now in the Blue Parlour

The Blue Parlour

Textiles

The 19th-century Aubusson carpet came from Markeaton Hall, the Derbyshire home of Fox Talbot's wife, Constance. It was given to Matilda Talbot by her sister-in-law, Harriet Clark–Maxwell.

The Painting Room

In the mid-19th century Fox Talbot's younger daughters, Rosamond and Matilda, used this room to finish their watercolours. Examples of their highly professional work, which include many views of Lacock, hang here.

The Cloisters in the early 19th century; by Nicholas Condy (Painting Room)

In the right-hand corner is the angled passage to the Tower Room.

The Tower Room

When you enter this room, you step straight back into Tudor Lacock.

It is William Sharington's most important surviving addition to the abbey, forming the first floor of a three-storey octagonal tower at the south-east corner of the building. For greater security, there was never any connecting staircase; indeed the top-floor banqueting room, which contains a similar, but damaged, table, can be entered only from the roof.

This room was designed as a strongroom, protected by a massive iron door. The walls are lined with recessed cupboards and stone shelves, supported by curling brackets of a kind that Sharington particularly liked. The rib-vaulted stone ceiling springs from similar brackets.

The room may seem cold and bare today, but you should visualise it filled with Sharington's precious books and other valuables, the most famous of which was the Lacock Magna Carta (see p. 19). Sharington also used the room as a study (the English equivalent of the Italian Renaissance *studiolo*), laying out his treasures to admire on the central table.

Furniture

The stone table is an extremely rare surviving piece of Tudor furniture. Even more unusually, it still occupies the room for which it was made.

The ideal Tudor strongroom, as defined by a follower of the Earl of Northumberland in the 1550s: 'A chamber very stronge and close, the walls should be of stone or bricke, the dore should be overplated with iron, the better to defend it from danger of fire… In this Chamber should be cubbards of drawing boxes, shelves and standards, with a convenient Table to write upon.'

The octagonal top matches the octagonal room and is supported by four grinning satyrs who wear acanthus-leaf skirts mirroring the acanthus-leaf capital in the centre. Above their horned heads are bunches of richly carved fruit. The base bears the ciphers of William Sharington and his third wife, Grace, which dates it to 1550–3.

The carving is of the very highest quality, influenced by advanced French and Italian Renaissance taste. It is attributed to the mason John Chapman, who also worked for Henry VIII, for John Dudley, Earl of Northumberland, and for Sharington's friend and neighbour at Longleat, Sir John Thynne.

Return to the Painting Room and turn right to reach the East Bedrooms.

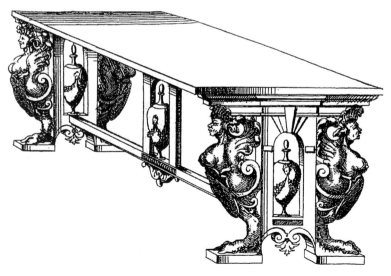

The stone table was inspired by engravings like this of c.1560 by the French designer Jacques Androuet Ducerceau

The stone table in the Tower Room

The Upper East and Ante Rooms

Sharington may have built these two small bed-rooms on to the outer wall of the nuns' former dormitory. Both are papered with mid-19th-century hand-printed wallpapers, which were conserved in 1995–6. The Chinoiserie paper in the Ante Room was made by Duppa, Slodden & Collins of Oxford Street, London.

Furniture

The beds are both early 19th-century, one painted in imitation of bamboo, the other French.

The Short Lobby

This small room occupies what was once part of the nuns' dormitory. The fine panelled door in the far right-hand corner probably came from another part of the house and may date back to Sharington's time.

The bookcases were moved here from the Blue Parlour after 1916.

Antiquities

The glass case in front of the window displays floor tiles glazed with Sharington's WS and scorpion cipher. Most of the other items were collected by Fox Talbot and testify to his wide interests. They include pot fragments dug up in the garden at Lacock, ancient Egyptian tablets and Ushabti (statuettes of servants placed in a mummy's tomb), and natural history specimens. *The leather overshoes* were worn by ponies while mowing the grass to prevent them from damaging the turf.

Pictures

Some of the earliest of the *family portraits* hang here. They include, flanking the door to the Stone Gallery, Olive Sharington (No. 50), dated

1580, and perhaps her son, Sharington Talbot the elder (No. 48), dated 1614 and attributed to Robert Peake. Olive inherited Lacock in 1581 and married her cousin, John Talbot of Salwarp, despite her father's initial objection. The historian of Wiltshire, John Aubrey, tells a tall tale of their romance:

Olive ... leaped, at night downe from the battlements of the Abbey Church, to Talbot, her lover, who caught her in his arms, but she struck him dead, and was with great difficulty brought to life: her father told her, 'Since she made such leaps, she should e'en marry him.'

Part of Fox Talbot's collection of natural history specimens is displayed in the Short Lobby

Watercolour of the Stone Gallery in 1914 by Matilda Gilchrist-Clark

The Stone Gallery

Sir William Sharington formed this broad gallery to offer views over the formal garden he created to the east of his house. Previously, it had been part of the nuns' dormitory. The stone fireplace, carved in Renaissance style, still survives from Sharington's time. It may have been the work of his mason, John Chapman. The interlace pattern on the hearth was created by pouring molten lead into the incised stonework. The broad windows are also largely Tudor, although the pointed Gothick tops were added by Ivory Talbot in the mid-18th century.

Stained glass and funeral helms

The fragments of medieval glass in the windows were collected and put here by Ivory Talbot. The early 17th-century helmets were tradition-ally carried in funeral processions. Two of them bear the Talbot lion crest.

Furniture

The six shell-backed chairs are of an Italian form known as *sgabello*. They were made in the 1630s, probably for Holland House in London by Franz Cleyn, an influential designer who also ran the royal tapestry works at Mortlake. Such chairs were often intended to stand in long galleries

---

The furnishings of the 'Long Stone Chamber' in 1575

1 counterpane of waterflower

4 hangings of waterflower

tester bed with taffeta hangings and swags

cupboard, chair, pair of fire irons

dornix [coarse damask] curtain, red saie curtain

---

like this and so were made in large sets. These ones have been repainted several times and now bear the Talbot rampant lion in the central cartouche on the back.

The large early 18th-century chest is inscribed BD for Barbara Davenport, Ivory Talbot's sister. *The Canadian moose horns* were probably acquired by William Davenport Talbot, who served in Canada in the late 18th century.

Pictures

The portraits include three-quarter-lengths of Ivory Talbot and his wife Mary by Michael Dahl (Nos 58 and 59).

The rocking horse was bought about 1840 by Fox Talbot for his children. It was one of the great joys of Matilda Talbot's childhood visits to Lacock: 'He was called Firefoot, because we said he galloped so fast that he struck fire from the stones in the road.'

Documents

The Lacock Magna Carta was given to the British Museum Library in 1946 and is represented here by a facsimile. It is one of only three surviving copies of the 1225 reissue of the 'Great Charter', a series of concessions wrung from an unwilling King John by a group of rebellious barons at Runnymede in Surrey in 1215. The King almost immediately went back on his word, but, in its definitive 1225 form, the Magna Carta became a powerful symbol of English liberty and of the rights of citizens everywhere to protection against arbitrary rule. The Lacock copy was probably given to Ela as High Sheriff of Wiltshire, and lodged for safety in the abbey library, where it remained for seven centuries.

(Left) One of the early 17th-century sgabello *chairs*

The Cloister Room

Sharington created this and the adjoining dressing room by partitioning the nuns' dormitory. As the name suggests, the windows overlook the medieval cloisters. These rooms are still used by the family as guest rooms and so are closed to visitors when occupied.

The wallpaper was made by Williams, Cooper & Boyle and bears a tax stamp for 1810. It was conserved in 1996. The curtains are in the art nouveau style of *c.*1900.

Pictures

Over the harpsichord is a portrait of Henry Davenport, who married Ivory Talbot's sister Barbara. Their grandson William Davenport Talbot inherited Lacock in 1790.

Furniture

The 17th-century x-framed armchair is upholstered with 18th-century floral needlework. It is said to have been converted from a camp chair used in Charles I's army.

The Brown Gallery

This gallery and the rooms leading off it on the right occupy the space of the nuns' medieval refectory (dining room). At the far end are two carved corbels, one of wood, the other of stone, that would have originally supported the refectory ceiling. In medieval times, the room was lit by round windows. The windows overlooking the cloister on the left were added by William Sharington.

On the end wall is a portrait of Matilda Talbot, who gave Lacock to the National Trust. It was painted in 1949 by her friend and neighbour at Corsham Court, Paul, Lord Methuen. He wrote the foreword to her memoirs, *My Life and Lacock Abbey*, in which he described her 'unchanging attitude of taking things as they come, but allowing events to shape her destiny through her confidence in human nature and in a spirit of harmony and goodwill'.

Taxidermy

Standing on top of a bookcase is *a stuffed pangolin*. The pangolin, or scaly ant-eater, is a native of south-east Asia. It uses a long sticky tongue to catch its prey, and its horny scales provide a good defence against predators. When threatened, a pangolin rolls up into a ball: its name comes from the Malayan word meaning 'rolling over'.

You return to the Hall by the passage at the far end of the room.

Metalwork

The bronze pestle and mortar are inscribed with William Sharington's name and scorpion cipher, and are recorded in the Kitchen in the 1575 inventory. They would have been used to grind herbs and spices.

Pictures

The portraits include Sir John Ivory (No. 81) and his wife, Anne Talbot (No. 82), who were the parents of John Ivory Talbot; and Henry Davenport (No. 76), who married Ivory Talbot's sister Barbara (No. 75).

Geological specimens acquired by Fox Talbot and his son Charles in the Brown Gallery

The exterior

Lacock is a fascinating mixture of the old, the new and the revived, sitting happily side-by-side. On the exterior, three main styles can be distinguished: medieval Gothic, Renaissance and 18th-century Gothick. From the outside, the building appears much larger than it really is, as it is set around a spacious central courtyard.

The west (entrance) front

No attempt was ever made to impose symmetry on Lacock. The lower range on the left contains the two Gothic windows of the medieval kitchen. In the centre is Ivory Talbot's Gothick entrance hall, reached by a double flight of stairs with a rose window above the central entrance doorway and flanked by two little cupolas on the roof. On the right is the much plainer end of the south range, which is relieved only by the two rectangular sash-windows of the early Georgian Dining Room.

The south front

The medieval abbey church stood on the lawn in front of this range. The buttress to the left of the three projecting oriel windows added by Fox Talbot in 1830 marks the north-west corner of the church, which was demolished in the 1540s. To the right is Sir William Sharington's octagonal tower. The house is at its shallowest on this side, comprising merely the south range of the cloisters, with the South Gallery above.

The east front

Much of the surviving wall is medieval, although the first-floor windows were gothicised by Ivory Talbot in the mid-18th century. The ground-floor stonework was restored in careful imitation of the original by Charles Talbot's architect, Sir Harold Brakspear, in the late 19th century. To the right is the long range of stables, haylofts and grooms' quarters built by Sir William Sharington. His chimney-stacks and heraldic beasts punctuate the skyline.

(Left)
William Sharington's octagonal tower connects the south and east fronts

(Right)
The west (entrance) front

(Overleaf) The Cloisters

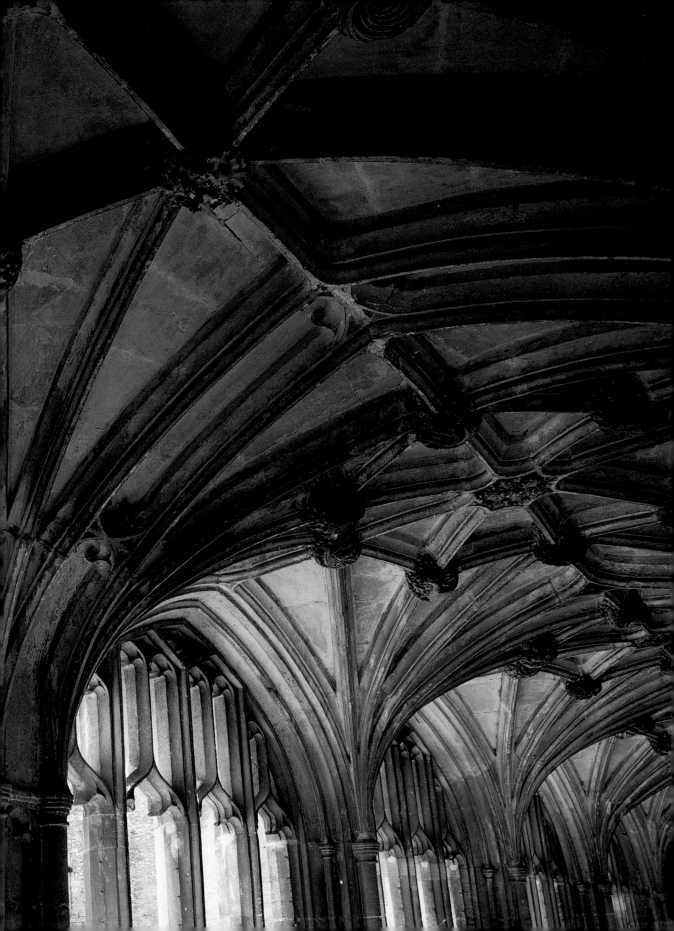

The Stable Court

Sharington laid out this service courtyard, which contains stables, bakehouse, dairy and brew-house on the ground floor, and haylofts on the first floor. It is said to have been built of stone salvaged from the demolished church. Although having a more humble function than the house, the Stable Court still preserves elegant Renaissance-style stone doorways.

The brew-house

This occupies two rooms to the right of the clock-tower. It is little changed since Sharington's time, apart from the brewing equipment, which remained in use until at least the 18th century. The smaller room contains the fireplace that heated the copper boiler which is set in a raised stone surround next door. The larger room also houses the cooling tray and the tun (shallow barrel), in which the beer was left to ferment.

How to brew beer

1. Heat water in copper to rolling boil.
2. Run off into mash tun below. Add malt and stir with wooden paddle for two hours.
3. Return mixture to copper, add hops and reheat.
4. Run off into cooling tray.
5. Drain into fermenting tun, and add yeast.
6. Leave for 2–7 days till fermentation complete.

Sculpture

Fixed to the wall are stone replicas of some of Sharington's mythical beasts, made while the detail in the originals is still visible, and awaiting the day when they have become dangerously eroded and must be replaced.

(Left)
The brew-house in
the Stable Court

(Above)
The brew-house

Replicas of the
Tudor carved stone
gargoyles are fixed to
the brew-house wall

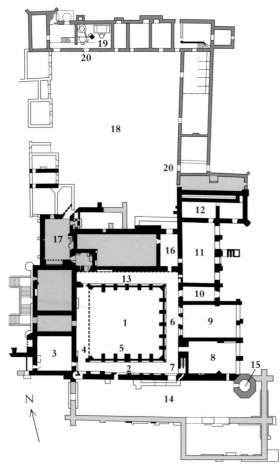

Plan of the medieval abbey and outbuildings

■ Monastic work

▨ Monastic work destroyed

■ 1540–53

□ Later

1	*Cloisters*	*11*	*Warming Room*
2	*South Cloister Walk*	*12*	*Storeroom*
3	*Chaplains' Room*	*13*	*North Cloister Walk*
4	*Ela's tomb*	*14*	*Monastic church*
5	*Masons' marks*	*15*	*Sharington's tower*
6	*East Cloister Walk*	*16*	*Parlour*
7	*Night Stair*	*17*	*Kitchen*
8	*Sacristy*	*18*	*Stable Court*
9	*Chapter-house*	*19*	*Brew-house*
10	*Infirmary Passage*	*20*	*Renaissance doorway*

The nunnery buildings

Many of the monasteries dissolved by Henry VIII in the 1530s were converted into country houses, but Lacock is highly unusual in preserving so many of the original rooms.

> 'Nothing could be more picturesque than the cloister, the elegant gothic arches of which are covered with ivy; the windows of our bedrooms are like nests of foliage.'
>
> Amélina Petit de Billier
> *August 1827*

1 The Cloisters

These would originally have run round all four sides of the courtyard, connecting the church to all the other elements of the abbey complex. Sharington converted the floor above into his living quarters. The traceried openings are all in the 15th-century Perpendicular style (the final phase of medieval Gothic), apart from two bays on the south side, which are in the 14th-century Decorated style.

The bosses in the cloister vaulting are carved with heraldic shields and a rich assortment of mythological and grotesque creatures. Ivory Talbot commissioned Lord William Seymour to paint them in the mid-18th century, but the present, somewhat crude colouring is mostly 19th-century.

2 The South Cloister Walk

Turn left and walk west to reach the Chaplains' Room. Just outside the door to this are the remains of the spiral staircase that would have been used by the abbess to reach her private quarters on the floor above. Her doorway into the church is now a window. Through the 'squint' (small opening) up the staircase, she could watch the nuns in the cloister.

(Above) The north and east sides of the Cloisters

(Left) A mermaid features in one of the decorative bosses in the Cloister vaulting

3 The Chaplains' Room

This would have been used by the abbey's three or four chaplains. About 70 per cent of the medieval plaster still survives here, despite the damage caused by the pipes from the 19th-century central-heating system.

The north wall is decorated with paintings of *St Christopher carrying the Christ Child, c.1275,* and *The Crucifixion of St Andrew,* 15th-century. On the same wall there are medieval graffiti depicting hares, nuns and grotesques, and signed *'Johan fecit hoc'* ('John did this'). On the east wall are the remains of a painted Crucifixion.

4 Ela's tomb The tombstone behind the iron railings is said to be that of Ela, Countess of

Late 13th-century mural of St Christopher in the Chaplains' Room

6 The East Cloister Walk

The ground floor of this range contains the most complete surviving set of medieval rooms at Lacock.

7 The Night Stair At the south end of this walk is a small lobby roofed with a ribbed vault. It contains the one remaining step of the night stair by which the nuns could reach the church direct from their dormitory.

8 The Sacristy In this room would have been kept the abbey's sacred vessels and vestments. It still retains a great deal of its original 13th-century plaster and limewashes. There are two cupboards in the west wall. A vault at the east end of the room is decorated with black six-rayed stars, which are thought to be late medieval. This may indicate that masses would have been said here for the souls of the dead. Beside it was probably another chapel with a doorway to the church, adjacent to which is still the original piscina (a basin for washing communion vessels). The outer wall and windows along this range were rebuilt in 1894 by Sir Harold Brakspear for Charles Talbot to a 13th-century Gothic design. Ivory Talbot had

Salisbury, the founder of the abbey. When she died in 1261, she was buried in front of the high altar of the church. After the church was demolished, her remains seem to have been reburied in the centre of the cloisters, from where they were moved to their present position in 1895. However, although the stone is old, it is not complete, and the inscription may be 18th-century. The Latin text can be translated: 'Below lie buried the bones of the venerable Ela, who gave this sacred house as a home for the nuns. She also lived here as holy abbess and countess of Salisbury, full of good works.'

5 Masons' marks In the tracery of the fourth archway on the north side of the South Cloister Walk you can see marks carved by the medieval masons to identify their work.

(Right) The cauldron made in 1500 is displayed in the Warming Room

demolished the original medieval walling in the mid-18th century.

9 The Chapter-house In this vaulted chamber the nuns would have held daily meetings to discuss abbey business. They would have sat at a continuous seat that once ran right round the room. Sharington inserted the fireplace. The tiles were laid in the 19th century at a level 10cm higher than the original.

10 The Infirmary Passage This corridor between the Chapter-house and the Warming Room led to the abbey hospital, all trace of which has now gone. Between the Infirmary Passage and the angle of the cloister are two recesses for books.

11 The Warming Room The nuns would have gathered here to get warm, as it was originally the only room with a fireplace. You reach it through a narrow passage in the north-east corner of the cloister, which may have been the Parlour (16) where visitors were received. *The stone coffins* in this room were excavated in the Chapter-house. To one side of the large hooded fireplace in the Warming Room, you can still see the remains of a lamp bracket. The window beyond the fireplace contains the original window seat.

The cauldron was made of bell metal, as the inscription records, in 1500 by Peter Wagheuens of Malines (modern Mechelen in Belgium). In the 19th century it stood out in the garden.

The tank was also brought in from outside, where it may have been used for washing raw wool or clothes, or simply for storing water or fish.

12 The Storeroom Fuel was stored here. Beyond the 15th-century wall is the main drain for the medieval garderobes (lavatories) on the floor above. Part of this drain was excavated in 2002 and is visible in the corner of the room.

13 The North Cloister Walk

This section of the cloister runs below what would have been the nuns' refectory (dining room). Restoration work in 1894 revealed a richly painted mural of a nun kneeling on a grassy mound receiving a blessing from a bishop saint, with a tree behind and a background covered with fleurs-de-lis. The inscription uncovered in 1984 dates the mural to the time of Agnes Frary, who was abbess at Lacock between 1429 and 1445. The saint is probably Augustine, the founder of the Order to which the Lacock nuns belonged. The mural was originally richly coloured, but the pigments have faded since it was revealed, and the wall surface is suffering from the very damp state of the old monastic rooms. The environment is being carefully monitored and a conservation plan implemented.

The North Cloister Walk

The garden

Lacock is essentially a Victorian woodland garden. In early spring, you first catch sight of the abbey through the trees across a carpet of common snowdrops and winter aconites. These are followed by purple, mauve and striped white crocuses, mainly *Crocus vernus*, which are descended from wild forms collected in Italy in the 1830s–'40s by Fox Talbot. Then come the flowering shrubs, which include viburnums, magnolia, philadelphus and forsythia. The meadow areas of the garden are not mown until July to allow the bulbs to set seed for the following season.

The early gardens

The nuns' garden was probably given over entirely to producing food, and seems to have been dominated by large fish-ponds. In the 1540s Sir William Sharington laid out garden courts to the east and south of the house, which were designed to be viewed from his new tower and were probably planted formally.

The 18th century

John Ivory Talbot made substantial alterations to the garden, the changing style of which mirrored his alterations to the house. He started in the 1720s by constructing a formal canal from a monastic stewpond (now a pool) and the terrace, which was separated from the park by a ha-ha. He also created an extensive formal garden north of the abbey, which consisted of straight, tree-lined paths and rides. At the head of the central ride he excavated the 'Great Basin' and at the opposite end set up the pair of Tuscan columns topped by a sphinx, which may have been carved by Benjamin Carter.

In 1753 Ivory Talbot commissioned Sanderson Miller to design the Gothick archway. 'Capability' Brown received £250 in

The drive is carpeted with crocuses and snowdrops in spring

A stone sphinx sits atop two Tuscan columns

best in June, include the ramblers 'Albéric Barbier' and 'François Juranville' and the shrub roses 'Penelope' and 'Jacques Cartier'.

Fox Talbot's Botanic Garden

As a student, Fox Talbot was already corresponding with leading botanists, and by the age of 29 he had been elected a fellow of the Linnean Society. He set aside a garden next to what is now the Fox Talbot Museum where he could pursue his botanical researches, which also inspired much of his pioneering photographic work (see p. 44). He travelled throughout Europe collecting rare specimens and formed a herbarium of plants from the Ionian Islands, which he bequeathed to Kew Gardens. Fox Talbot was particularly fond of alpines and bulbs, which he planted informally under the rare specimen trees he introduced to the pleasure ground. He also collected euphorbias and orchids. His two step-sisters and his three daughters each had their own garden.

Fox Talbot's son Charles was more interested in the house than the garden and seems to have allowed his father's botanic garden to fall into decline. By the time Lacock passed to the National Trust in 1944, it had become allotments for the village.

The garden today

The National Trust is gradually restoring the garden to reflect its character in Fox Talbot's time. Using a late 19th-century estate map, it has plotted the positions of the flower-beds, paths, summer-house and glasshouses in his botanic garden. This garden was reopened in 2000 to mark the 200th anniversary of Fox Talbot's birth. The 26-metre-long glasshouses where Fox Talbot carried out propagation experiments and housed many of his plant collections were built in the second quarter of the 19th century, altered in the late 19th century and diminished in the 1950s. In 2004 work began on rebuilding them. Elsewhere, the beds and borders have all been planted up with species that interested Fox Talbot, including campanulas, euphorbias, phlomis and eryngium.

1755–6 for unspecified work in the park. This may have included creating the present drive, which gives a first tantalising glimpse of the abbey before disappearing into woodland and re-emerging to offer a view of the entrance front carefully framed by Miller's new archway.

Lady Elisabeth's Rose Garden

Fox Talbot's mother, Lady Elisabeth, came from a family of gardeners, her brother William creating a famous arboretum at Abbotsbury in Dorset. About 1829–31 she laid out the rose garden, which was centred on an urn surrounded by iron arches linked with metal strips. The National Trust restored her design in the early 1990s. The roses, which are at their

The village

Lacock today is a pretty village, but until the late 19th century it was a busy industrial town – a place of work.

The ancient settlement of Lacock (which means 'small stream' in Anglo-Saxon) enjoyed its greatest prosperity with the rise of the West Country wool trade in the 14th and 15th centuries, when the grid pattern of the four main streets – High, Church, East and West – was laid out. Thanks to its excellent links by road and river, Lacock became a thriving centre for local trade, focused on the weekly markets and annual fair. A market cross still stands in the school playground. Visitors were fed and watered by the town's many inns, the oldest of which is the George in West Street. Prosperity also paid for the rebuilding of the church, which bears an unusual dedication, to St Cyriac, a Roman boy martyred in the 3rd century AD.

Fleeces from the abbey's flocks, which grazed the surrounding downs, were washed in the River Avon. The wool was then woven into cloth on the broadlooms that filled the spacious first-floor rooms of many of the houses in Lacock. Most of the townspeople were tenants of the abbey and so were obliged to pay it a tithe of corn, hides and fleeces, which were stored in the massive 14th-century tithe barn on the corner of East and High Streets.

With the gradual decline of the wool trade in the late 18th century, the townspeople turned to other trades, principally tanning, which took place in an open barn in an area still known as the tanyard. There was also work constructing

The George Inn

the new railways during the boom of the 1840s. But times were often hard, and many were forced to leave Lacock or be taken into the workhouse, built in the 1830s.

Despite the loss of so much work, in the early 20th century Lacock still supported a wide range of different trades – chair-maker, carpenter, wheelwright, coal merchant, miller, baker, and two blacksmiths. Although the Talbots cherished the physical fabric of Lacock, they were unable to protect these businesses from market forces, and they have all now gone. But Lacock still has a grocer, post office and three pubs, and, most important of all, its own school.

A separate guide describes the history of the village in greater detail.

(Left) The medieval tithe barn

Peggy Butler remembers food-shopping in Lacock in the early 20th century

'I remember the baking being done by the late John Horwood. He had one of the old wood fagot ovens where he baked a really crusty loaf; when you cut it the crust flew in all directions. He made a most delicious dough cake, and lardy cakes with a thick honey concoction on the bottom, full of fruit. He was rather erratic in his delivery, one day you would get your bread in the evening and next day, first thing in the morning. There was a pork butchers shop in the High Street, Colletts, where we used to be able to get hot baked faggots, chitterlings, pigs trotters and tripe. People would go along there at dinner time with their plates and get a meal of hot faggots. You could get four faggots for 6d.

Mr Taylor who lived at the old Cruck House, used to sell home-made ice cream. You got a huge cornet for 1d or a thick sandwich for 2d.'

*The Lacock Magna
Carta*

*The medieval seal of
Lacock Abbey*

Ela, Countess of Salisbury (d. 1261)
Founding the nunnery

The nunnery of Lacock Abbey was founded on the morning of 16 April 1232 by Ela, Countess of Salisbury. The same afternoon she rode sixteen miles to found a charterhouse at Hinton. Ela was Countess of Salisbury in her own right and one of the most powerful women of the Middle Ages. She had been brought up at court as a ward of Richard I. While still a child, she was married to William Longespée, the natural son of Henry II and his mistress, the 'fair Rosamund' Clifford, and so Richard's half-brother. Like Richard, William spent much of his life abroad on crusade. Despite numerous reports of his death, which encouraged suitors to pursue Ela for her money, she refused to give up hope that he would return. Her faithfulness was rewarded, and he did finally return. During the reign of King John, William was one of the great barons that forced the King to sign the Magna Carta limiting his powers. With Ela, he helped to found Salisbury Cathedral in 1220, and it was here that he was commemorated with an ornate tomb after his death in 1226.

Ela kept William's heart to bury at Lacock, which she founded in his memory. She chose a site between the village of Lacock and the River Avon, where she built a church from the local Haslebury limestone and from royal oaks given by Henry III.

Lacock was dedicated to the Virgin Mary and St Bernard (both of whom appear on the abbey's seal) and was served at first by fifteen nuns of the Augustinian Order. In 1238 Ela decided to give up the worldly life and join her nuns, and three years later she became Lacock's first abbess. When she died in 1261, she was buried beneath the high altar of her church.

Lacock remained a small, but wealthy, religious community throughout the Middle Ages. Most of its nuns came from well-to-do families to be educated at Lacock and to observe the Order's rule of obedience and chastity. They dressed in a tunic of white wool and a mantle lined with white cloth in summer and fur in winter. They also wore a fur pilch (cloak), veil

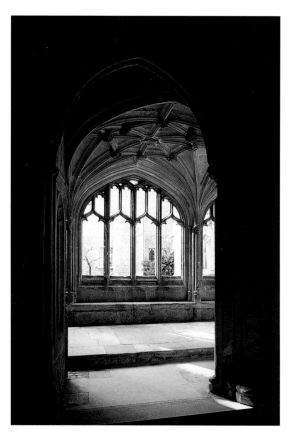

and wimple. The abbey took in those in need and offered a daily dole of food and drink to the local poor. Thanks to Ela's royal connections, Lacock was granted a weekly market and an annual three-day fair. It also enjoyed the income from a large estate, which included a flock of over 2,000 sheep in 1476. The nuns' diet depended heavily on mutton and fish. They ate salted herrings in large quantities during Lent and on days of abstinence. The fishery in the nearby Avon also supplied them with freshwater fish and eels.

Lacock Abbey's life of prayer and charity continued until 1535, when it was first inspected by the King's Commissioners, who were charged with rooting out corruption in the ancient monasteries. They were unable to find fault with the regime at Lacock: the nuns were scrupulously following the rules of their order, there was no disorder, and they had an adequate income for their work. The abbey escaped with a fine. But despite a later report that the nuns were 'of vertuous lyving and desyring to continue religios', the abbey was suppressed in 1539 in the final wave of monastic dissolutions. The nuns were pensioned off, and the lead stripped from the roof. Three centuries of religious life had come to an end.

(Left top)
The abbey cloister

(Left)
A carved head surviving from the medieval abbey in the Brown Gallery

(Right)
The tomb of Ela's husband, William Longespée, in whose memory she founded the abbey

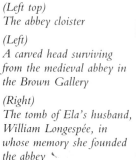

Sir William Sharington
(c.1495–1553)
From nunnery to Tudor country house

Sir William Sharington was one of the ambitious new men who transformed Tudor England. He played for high stakes and lost, but still managed to survive.

Sharington came from a minor Norfolk gentry family and rose to power as a protégé of Sir Thomas Seymour, the brother of Henry VIII's third Queen, Jane Seymour. In July 1540 he bought the dissolved abbey of Lacock for £782, rapidly accumulating a large estate in Wiltshire, which was the centre of Seymour power. Sharington financed his land purchases through moneylending and foreign trade from the port of Bristol. In 1546 he was appointed under-treasurer of the Bristol mint, where he enriched himself still further by illegally clipping the coins it issued. The following year marked the summit of Seymour power, when Sir Thomas's nephew was crowned King Edward VI. His elder brother Edward became the boy-king's chief minister and effectively the supreme ruler of England. Sharington's reward was a knighthood. But Sir Thomas Seymour, who envied his brother's power, overreached himself by attempting to marry the Princess Elizabeth. In January 1549 Sir Thomas was arrested on a charge of conspiring against his brother and sent to the Tower of London. Sharington was rounded up with him. Investigators were sent to Lacock, where they seized papers, cash and jewels and uncovered Sharington's Bristol fraud. He admitted embezzling £4,000 over three years, and in February 1549 was tried and convicted: his estates were confiscated, and he was condemned to death. Sharington managed to escape execution by giving evidence against Sir Thomas Seymour, and when Edward Seymour also fell from power the following November, he was pardoned and retrieved his estates. By 1552, the year before he died, Sharington had restored his position sufficiently to be appointed Sheriff of Wiltshire.

Turning the abbey into a country house entailed demolishing the church to the south of the cloisters. Sharington also sold the church bells to pay for rebuilding Rae bridge in a new

Sir William Sharington; portrait attributed to Anthonis Mor (South Gallery)

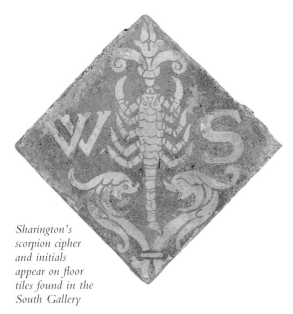

Sharington's scorpion cipher and initials appear on floor tiles found in the South Gallery

position that took the main road away from his house. He preserved the cloisters as a central courtyard, creating a series of connecting galleries and apartments on the floor above. This novel arrangement anticipates that at nearby Longleat, although Sharington made no attempt to impose external symmetry on the result. Of his additions, the most interesting, and least altered, is the octagonal tower, which served as strongroom, banqueting house and viewing platform for his formal garden. The stone to build it probably came from the ruins of Devizes Castle, then owned by Sir Thomas Seymour.

Sharington was an unattractive, but deeply cultured man. His portrait was drawn by Holbein (facsimile on show in the South Gallery). The two stone tables he commissioned for the tower are in the most advanced Renaissance style, which was favoured by the Seymour and Dudley circles at court. They are probably based on Flemish Renaissance engravings printed in Antwerp, then the cultural capital of northern Europe, with which Sharington had strong trading ties. To make the tables and chimneypieces, he turned to John Chapman, one of the best stone carvers in England, whom he generously recommended to his friend and neighbour at Longleat, Sir John Thynne. So close were the links between the two families that in the 1570s a room was named after Lady Thynne at Lacock. Chapman also carved chimneypieces for the Dudleys during his stay at Lacock. It was entirely appropriate that, after Sharington died in 1553, he should be remembered with a canopied tomb in Lacock church which is a masterpiece of the Renaissance style and the stone-mason's art.

(Right top) Sharington's Renaissance tomb monument in Lacock church

(Right) The upper room of Sharington's tower houses a stone table similar to that on display in the room below

The early Talbots

Sharington married three times, but had no children, so the estate passed in 1553 to his younger brother Henry. Henry consolidated his position by marrying Anne Paget, a daughter of Sir William's third wife by a former husband, and they lived quietly at Lacock for the next 28 years. Life at Lacock in that era can be reconstructed from an inventory drawn up in 1575. The Wardrobe Chamber was packed with richly embroidered chairs and cushions, silk quilts and a large Turkey carpet, which were doubtless brought out for special occasions. The greatest of these happened in September 1574, when Queen Elizabeth visited Lacock during a progress from Bristol to Wilton. Henry was knighted by the Queen that day, and commemorated the visit by naming a room in her honour.

Sir Henry Sharington had four children. His only son William died in infancy, but his three daughters were all married well, Ursula to Thomas Sadleir, the son of the builder of Sutton House in east London (also the property of the National Trust). Sir Henry seems to have initially refused permission for his daughter and heir Olive to marry John Talbot of Salwarp, who was a descendant of Ela, Countess of Salisbury, but then relented (see p. 17). To preserve the family name, Olive christened their son Sharington, but she outlived him, handing on the estate to her grandson, who was also named Sharington.

The Civil War and Restoration

The Talbots supported the King during the Civil War, when Lacock was occupied by a royalist garrison. After the fall of Bristol and Devizes to the Parliamentary forces in 1645, Sharington Talbot was forced to surrender the abbey to General Fairfax. When the war was over, he was also fined £1,000.

Sharington Talbot's younger brother Gilbert kept the royalist cause alive during the Commonwealth by helping to set up what

Olive Sharington, who inherited Lacock in 1581 (Short Lobby)

Sharington Talbot the Elder; attributed to Robert Peake, 1614 (Short Lobby)

Sir Gilbert Talbot; by John Hayls

with the 2nd Duke of Buckingham, who had seduced the Earl's wife. Samuel Pepys described what happened:

My Lord Shrewsbury is run through the body from the right breast through the shoulder, and Sir Jo. Talbot all along up one of his arms and Jenkins [Buckingham's second] killed upon the place, and the rest all in a little measure wounded. This will make the world think that the King hath good councillors about him, when the Duke of Buckingham, the greatest man about him, is a fellow of no more sobriety than to fight about a whore.

Shrewsbury eventually died of his wounds, but Sir John recovered. This narrow escape seems to have taught Sir John's son Sharington very little. For in 1685 he fought an even more pointless, and fatal, duel. Having served very bravely with the Wiltshire militia at the battle of Sedgmoor, he got caught up in an argument with another militia officer over whose men had fought better. Tempers became so heated that swords were drawn, and Talbot was killed. His sudden death ended the male Talbot line at Lacock.

became the Sealed Knot, a secret society plotting the return of Charles II. When his involvement in the conspiracy was revealed, he was thrown into Gloucester jail. On his release, he fled to France to join Charles II's exiled court and was delighted when the King was restored to power in 1660. He was elected a founder member of the Royal Society, but like many royalists who had suffered for their loyalty, he found it impossible to get any compensation for his financial losses. As a result, at the end of his long life he was obliged to settle at Lacock with his nephew Sir John Talbot, who had inherited in 1677.

Sir John Talbot was involved in one of the most famous duels in British history. In January 1668 he acted as a second to his Talbot cousin, the Earl of Shrewsbury, when he fought a duel

The entrance front of Lacock in 1684; from Thomas Dingley's History from Marble

John Ivory Talbot (?1691–1772)
Gothick Lacock

On Sir John Talbot's death in 1714 Lacock passed to his eldest grandson by his second wife, the 23-year-old John Ivory, who changed his name to Talbot to acknowledge the source of his good fortune. Over the next 58 years he was to transform Lacock.

He began, conventionally enough, by remodelling the Dining Room in a plain classical style. But in 1753 he was introduced to the gentleman-architect Sanderson Miller by a mutual friend, Richard Goddard, who commented: 'As his house consists of the Remains of an Old Nunnery it was agreed on all Hands, that it would be most proper to fit it up in the Gothick Taste.' Miller himself probably also had a say in the decision, as he was a pioneering advocate of the new Gothick style. Miller designed a new approach to Lacock through a Gothick arch and also rebuilt the abbey's west front around a new Gothick hall. Much of the detail was taken from Batty Langley's influential book, *Antient Architecture Restored* (1741–2).

Ivory Talbot got on famously with Miller, who praised his client as 'a very agreeable companion'. He also appreciated the skill of his stonemasons and looked after them, making sure that the hall roof was on before winter set in, so that they would not have to work out in the cold. He was delighted with all their efforts, celebrating the completion of the hall with a huge party, to which he invited all those friends and relations commemorated on the heraldic ceiling.

Ivory Talbot seems to have got on less well with his wife, the heiress Mary Mansel of Margam in Glamorgan, whose trying behaviour is said to have driven him to

(Right top) John Ivory Talbot, who remodelled Lacock in the Gothick style

(Right) The heiress Mary Mansel, who married Ivory Talbot

Sanderson Miller (1716–80), champion of the Gothick style

Miller was the squire of Radway Grange in Warwickshire, which overlooked the Civil War battlefield of Edgehill. The historical resonances of the place inspired him to build an octagonal tower overlooking it in a deliberately backward-looking Gothic style. Miller's talent for designing sham castles and ready-made ruins found a receptive audience among country-house owners keen to fill their gardens with follies that evoked history. In Ivory Talbot he found a client who shared his passion for the past.

drink. Despite this, there remained close links for several generations between the Talbots of Lacock and their Welsh cousins at Margam, who gave their name to the docks at Port Talbot.

The Davenport Talbots

Ivory Talbot's only son John died childless in 1778, passing Lacock to his sister Martha, who had married her cousin, the Rev. William Davenport. Their son, William Davenport Talbot, was commissioned into the Dragoons, with which he served in Canada. He married Lady Elisabeth Fox-Strangways, the daughter of the 2nd Earl of Ilchester, but died shortly afterwards in 1800. He left behind an estate deep in debt, but also a five-month-old son, who was to be the most remarkable person ever to live at Lacock.

Ivory Talbot's son and heir, John Talbot; painted in the 1760s by Thomas Gainsborough

William Henry Fox Talbot (1800–77)

Pioneer of photography

The dominant influence on William Henry's early life was his mother, Lady Elisabeth Fox-Strangways. From her he inherited his surname, his fascination with botany and his facility for languages (his scientific papers are written in a mixture of English, French, Italian and Latin). Because of debts, in 1800 his mother decided to leave Lacock, which was rented out, first to a Talbot cousin, Lady Shrewsbury, and then to J. R. Grosett, the MP for Chippenham. Henry endured a nomadic childhood until 1804, when his mother married Captain Charles Feilding, who presented him with two half-sisters.

Fox Talbot began to display his genius for science at Harrow school, where he published *The Flora and Fauna of Harrow* (1811) with his friend Walter Calverley Trevelyan of Wallington. At Trinity College, Cambridge, he won prizes for both classics and maths and was publishing learned papers even before he had

William Henry Fox Talbot; from a daguerreotype made by Antoine Claudet about 1845–6

taken his MA. In 1824 he met the astronomer John Herschel, who encouraged his research into optics. Herschel in turn introduced him to the Scottish scientist Dr David Brewster, who was to be an equally important influence.

Fox Talbot finally returned to Lacock in 1827, after his step-father had painstakingly restored the family finances. Little had been done to the house since the 1750s, and so, with the encouragement of Constance Mundy, whom he married in 1832, he put in hand a programme of modernisation which included remodelling the South Gallery. He was also committed to political change, being elected to Parliament in 1831 as a reform candidate.

In October 1833 he was honeymooning by Lake Como in northern Italy, when he became frustrated by his inability to record the picturesque scenery with the same artistic skill as his wife and sisters: 'How charming it would be if it were possible to cause these natural images to imprint themselves durably, and remain fixed upon the paper.' From this frustration, photography was born. In the spring of 1834 Fox Talbot started experimenting at Lacock by coating sheets of paper with a solution of salt and silver nitrate. He found that when opaque objects such as fern leaves or lace were placed on the treated paper and exposed to the sun's rays, a silhouette of them was left behind on the paper. He christened his invention 'photogenic drawing'. He also discovered how to 'fix' these images with a wash of potassium iodide and conceived the idea of the 'negative' image, from which multiple 'positive' prints could be reproduced. However, he was distracted by other responsibilities from publishing these fundamental discoveries. It was, for instance, largely thanks to his efforts in 1838 that Kew Gardens were saved from closure and established as the national plant collection.

In January 1839 Fox Talbot was alarmed to read newspaper reports that the French scene painter Louis Daguerre had managed to preserve images captured by a *camera obscura*. Fox Talbot rushed to show examples of his own work to the Royal Society, but in a sunless winter he was unable to replicate his first experiments. Daguerre received public recognition as the

'The Fruit Sellers' was photographed in the Cloisters. Many of Fox Talbot's calotypes include views of the abbey

'father of photography' and lavish financial support from the French government for his work. Fox Talbot got nothing. Despite these disappointments, he continued to refine his invention in 1839–40. His first cameras consisted of a microscope lens and a crude wooden box built by the Lacock carpenter, which required a very long exposure to capture an image (his wife nicknamed them 'mousetraps'). He discovered that he could reduce exposure times by treating the exposed paper with a chemical 'developer', which would strengthen the latent image. He christened the result the calotype, declining the alternative title 'talbotype' suggested by his friends. The daguerreotype initially bested the calotype, as its greater clarity was more suited to portraiture, which was the mainstay of the new medium, but because the calotype could generate multiple images from a single original, it was ultimately to have much greater commercial potential. Fox Talbot encouraged his valet Nicolaas Henneman to open a commercial photographic works in Reading in 1843. In June 1844 he also started publishing *The Pencil of Nature*, illustrated with calotypes of

Lacock. The photographic book had arrived. Unfortunately, he had to endure lawsuits when the patents he had taken out were challenged. Dismayed by public controversy, he abandoned his research, and his health suffered. He did not return to this work again until the 1850s, when he developed a more reliable process for reproducing photographs with printer's ink by engraving them on a steel printing plate. All the modern techniques of photogravure printing can be traced back to this invention.

Fox Talbot is remembered today as a pioneer of photography, but his interests spread much wider. In his later years, he devoted himself to unravelling the mysteries of Assyrian cuneiform. He was also a classicist, geologist, mathematician, physicist, botanist and astronomer. And Lacock itself, the subject of so many of his photographs, was not forgotten: one of his daughters was christened Ela after the founder of the abbey; another, Rosamond, after Ela's mother-in-law.

Fox Talbot's achievements are explored further in the Fox Talbot Museum and in a separate guide.

Charles Talbot

Charles Talbot (1842–1916)
A scholar-squire

Life at Lacock in the 40 years after Fox Talbot's death in 1877 was a great deal quieter. His only son and heir, Charles, was the epitome of the shy Victorian scholar-squire. According to his niece, Matilda Talbot, he was 'tall and thin and he walked rather slowly with a slight stoop'. In his youth, he had wanted to be an architect, but had had to abandon this career because of poor health. However, he remained fascinated by old buildings, and particularly by Lacock, about which he wrote many learned articles. He also commissioned Sir Harold Brakspear to restore the medieval remains of the abbey, removing many of John Ivory Talbot's less scholarly alterations. He devoted equal attention to the village, ensuring that its ancient buildings were repaired using traditional methods, and that new work was in sympathy with the old.

Charles Talbot preferred to spend money on the estate rather than on himself. As a result, his clothes were usually somewhat shabby. Always a poor sleeper, he went to bed early and rose late, often not coming down to breakfast until 11.30. He was fond of cats.

Charles Talbot never married and when his health began to fail in the late 19th century, he asked his unmarried sister Rosamond to come and look after him at Lacock. There were then only two indoor servants, elderly sisters who acted as cook and housekeeper. (Charles's father had employed a staff of nine.) With Rosamond came her young niece Matilda.

Matilda Talbot (1871–1958)
Preserving Lacock

Matilda Gilchrist-Clark never dreamt that she would inherit Lacock. She was brought up on the Drumlanrig estate in Dumfries, where her father was agent to the Duke of Buccleuch. On a first visit to Lacock in 1877, she met her grandfather, Henry Fox Talbot, remembered as a kind and friendly old gentleman, who let her look through his microscope. She shared his love of travel and talent for languages. Matilda trained as a cookery teacher, and although her favourite aunt Rosamond encouraged her to stay at Lacock, it came as a complete shock when she discovered that her uncle Charles had left her the entire Lacock estate on his death in 1916. Despite her new responsibilities, Matilda Talbot (as she became in 1918) volunteered for war work, serving food to exhausted French soldiers in Alsace. She later joined the Wrens.

Matilda Talbot on the 1932 Lacock Pageant

'We had come to the conclusion that all those taking part should be people belonging to the village or their friends ... that everybody should be shown engaged in his own trade, the blacksmith should be a blacksmith, the shepherd a shepherd and so forth.... In this way there should be a certain reality about everyone, both in their appearance and their behaviour.'

Matilda Talbot in her costume as Ela, Countess of Salisbury for the 1932 Lacock Pageant

She was fascinated by the history of Lacock and conscious of her duties towards all those who lived and worked on the estate. The high-light of the interwar years was perhaps the pageant held in 1932 to commemorate the 700th anniversary of the foundation of the abbey. With advice from the medieval historian Eileen Power, she recreated the events of the foundation day in meticulous detail, herself taking the role of the founder, Ela, Countess of Salisbury, in purple mantle and gold coronet. The pageant attracted an audience of 10,000. She appreciated the importance of Lacock's historic archive, generously giving its greatest treasure, the Lacock Magna Carta, to the British Museum Library in 1946, and many of Fox

Talbot's photographs to the Science Museum (now transferred to the National Museum of Photography, Film and Television in Bradford).

During the Second World War, 85 children from St George's, Campden Hill in London were evacuated to Lacock. The South Gallery became their schoolroom and survived the experience unscathed – to Matilda Talbot's great relief and pleasure. She never married and became increasingly concerned to secure the historic integrity of Lacock for the future. She first considered setting up a women's college at Lacock in the spirit of the original foundation. Her aunt Rosamond had been a great admirer of Octavia Hill, which may have encouraged her to give the abbey, village and estate to the National Trust in 1944.

In her memoirs, Matilda Talbot expressed the hope that Lacock 'may adapt itself to all the changes through which we are living, so as to preserve this spirit sympathetically enough to reach and touch contemporary thought.' The National Trust endeavours to fulfil her wishes.

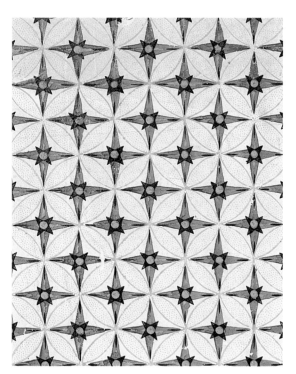

The early 19th-century wallpaper in the Cloister Room was conserved in 1996

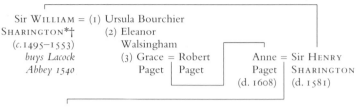

Sharington

Talbot

Sir WILLIAM = (1) Ursula Bourchier
SHARINGTON*† (2) Eleanor
(c.1495–1553) Walsingham
buys Lacock (3) Grace = Robert   Anne = Sir HENRY
Abbey 1540 Paget | Paget   Paget | SHARINGTON
                              (d. 1608) (d. 1581)

OLIVE SHARINGTON* = (1) John Talbot (d. 1581) m. 1574
(d. 1646) (2) Sir Robert Stapilton (d. 1606) m. 1584

Sharington Talbot of Salwarp* = (1) Elizabeth Leighton*
(d. 1642) (2) Mary Washbourne

SHARINGTON TALBOT = Jane Lyttleton   Sir Gilbert Talbot, FRS   Earls of Shrewsbury
of Salwarp and Lacock   (c.1606–95)
(d. 1677)

Sir JOHN TALBOT*† = (1) Elizabeth Keyte (d. 1656) m. 1653   Elizabeth = Henry Davenport
(1630–1714) (2) Barbara Slingsby* m. 1660   (d. 1698)

Sharington = Anne   Anne* = Sir John Ivory*   Barbara* = Viscount de   Gilberta*
Talbot Lawley   (1665–1720) | of New Ross, Co. Wexford   Longueville*
(1656–85) m. 1683   (1655–95)

John Ivory = Mary*, dau. of Lord Mansel   (2) Barbara* = Henry Davenport* = (1) Mary   Gen. Sharington
TALBOT* | of Margam   (d. 1748) (1677–1731) | Chardin*   Davenport*
(?1691–1772)   (d. 1719)

John Talbot* = Elizabeth Stone   MARTHA = Rev. William   Sharington = Gratiana   Mary = John
(?1717–78) m. 1742   TALBOT | Davenport*   Davenport* Rodd*   Elizabeth* Mytton
                             d. 1790 (d. 1781)   (d. 1744)

(1) WILLIAM DAVENPORT TALBOT = Lady Elisabeth Fox-Strangways* = (2) Admiral Charles Feilding (1780–1837)
(1764–1800) (1773–1846) m. 1804
dau. of 2nd Earl of Ilchester

WILLIAM HENRY FOX TALBOT* = Constance Mundy   Caroline = Ernest, 3rd Earl of   Horatia
(1800–77) (1811–80) m. 1832   (1808–81) Mount Edgcumbe   (1810–51)

CHARLES HENRY TALBOT   Ela Theresa   Rosamond Constance   Matilda Caroline = John Gilchrist-Clark
(1842–1916) (d. 1893)   (d. 1906)   (d. 1927)

William Gilchrist Clark-Maxwell = Harriet Alice Selwyn   MATILDA THERESA*
(1865–1935) (1867–1957)   *assumed* TALBOT *name 1918*
                             (1871–1958)
                             presented Lacock to
Katharine Mary = Alexander Burnett-Brown   *National Trust 1944*
(1898–1971) (1894–1966)

Janet   Anthony = Petronella Dittmer   * denotes a portrait on show in the house
b. 1927   (1930–2002) (b. 1948)   † denotes a monument in the church